Fake News

What Are Satire and Parody?

Matt Doeden

Lerner Publications ◆ Minneapolis

Lerner Publications Company
An Imprint of Lerner Publishing Group, Inc.
241 First Avenue North
Minneapolis, MN 55401 USA

For reading levels and more information, look up this title at www.lernerbooks.com.

Main body text set in Adrianna Regular.
Typeface provided by Chank.

Library of Congress Cataloging-in-Publication Data

Names: Doeden, Matt.
Title: What are satire and parody? / Matt Doeden.
Description: Minneapolis : Lerner Publications, [2020] | Series: Searchlight books. Fake news | Includes bibliographical references and index.
Identifiers: LCCN 2019005181 (print) | LCCN 2019011386
    (ebook) | ISBN 9781541556690 (eb pdf) | ISBN 9781541555792 (lb : alk. paper) |
    ISBN 9781541574748 (pb : alk. paper)
Subjects: LCSH: Satire—History and criticism—Juvenile literature. | Parody—Juvenile
    literature. | Fake news—Juvenile literature.
Classification: LCC PN6149.S2 (ebook) | LCC PN6149.S2 D64 2020 (print) | DDC
    809.7—dc23

LC record available at https://lccn.loc.gov/2019005181

Manufactured in the United States of America
1-46034-43357-5/3/2019

Contents

PAGE PLUS! Scan QR codes throughout for more content!

Chapter 1

SATIRE AND PARODY

The 2000 US presidential election was a tight race between George W. Bush and Al Gore. The campaign included many big moments. But one that never happened in real life became famous.

Al Gore (*left*) and George W. Bush (*right*) debated at the University of Massachusetts in October 2000.

On *Saturday Night Live*, Darryl Hammond (*left*) and Will Ferrell (*right*) made fun of the presidential debate in a comedy skit.

It happened on the TV show *Saturday Night Live*. A skit poked fun at a debate between the two candidates. Actor Darryl Hammond played Gore as a stuffy know-it-all. Will Ferrell played Bush as a person who could never find the right words. Most famously, he summed up his campaign in a made-up word: *strategery*. Almost two decades later, the fake debate remains part of popular culture.

The skit was an example of both satire and parody. It highlighted the politicians' actual strengths and weaknesses.

What Is Satire?

Satire is a style of writing or performance that makes fun of a person or idea. Satire usually is meant to be funny. It looks at something or someone in a silly or ironic way. Satire may be comical, but it often has another purpose. It is social or political criticism. Many writers and performers use satire as a way to spark social change.

In 2014, President Barack Obama (*left*) appeared on *The Colbert Report*, a popular satirical television show.

For example, a popular social media meme shows a cartoon of a lecture hall. A dry-erase board identifies the lecture as "Climate Science Deniers." A speaker behind a podium speaks to a single audience member. It's a skeleton. The skeleton says, "You don't have to be right . . . just create doubt!" The cartoon mocks people who deny modern climate science. This causes people to feel more strongly about global climate change.

What Is Parody?

Parody is a type of satire. It imitates a person or idea using exaggerated traits of that person or idea. Parody, sometimes called a spoof, is usually comical. Parody can have a social message, but it's mainly for entertainment.

A caricature is a drawing that parodies a person's look, like this one of President Bill Clinton.

"WEEKEND UPDATE" PARODIES REAL NEWS STORIES IN A FUNNY WAY.

Parody comes in many forms. It's in books, poems, movies, and TV shows. *Saturday Night Live* is one of the most popular shows to use parody. Many of its parody skits are lighthearted. One is the popular "Weekend Update" skit. It is a parody of news programs. It makes fun of how news is delivered. It looks at a wide range of current events.

Stories in the *Onion* range from ridiculous to almost sounding real.

Both parody and satire are meant to be funny. But sometimes they're a little too realistic and become fake news. Sometimes, a satirical story in a publication such as the *Onion* (a satirical newspaper) is shared on social media. This can confuse some of the people who read it. They think it's real news even though it's all made up. Satire and parody rarely are made to deceive people. But they can be misunderstood.

Real or Fake?

Is this story real or fake? See the Fake News
Toolkit on page 29 to help you decide.

Justin Bieber
@justinbieber

My dear beliebers I'm retiring from music.

9:00 PM - December 24, 2013

 1   1   1

Real! Pop star Justin Bieber announced his retirement from music in a
post similar to this. He went on to say that he was frustrated with how
the media covered him. Of course, Bieber quickly changed his mind. But
the post was real, much to the shock of Bieber fans. How can you tell?
A quick internet search will reveal that this is Bieber's true Twitter
account, and media outlets quickly picked up the story.

Chapter 2

A HISTORY OF SATIRE

Satire has been around throughout human history. An early example is the *Satire of the Trades*. This text comes from ancient Egypt. The writing shows a father talking to his son. He tells his son that becoming a scribe (a person who records information) will be his best choice in life. He does so by describing other trades, or jobs. He makes them sound so terrible that being a scribe sounds great.

A tablet from the *Satire of the Trades* is on exhibit at the Louvre Museum in Paris, France.

Roman emperors such as Marcus Aurelius could be criticized only through satire.

The writings of ancient Egypt, Greece, and Rome were filled with satire. The ancient Romans were famous for making political satire. They even created the word *satire*. Roman emperors did not like criticism. So the Roman people hid their criticisms in stories using satire.

The Evolution of Satire

Satire varied from culture to culture. When dictators ruled, the meaning was often hidden. In more open

societies, such as England and France in the sixteenth century, the meaning was more direct. One of the most famous satirical writers then was François Rabelais. He challenged French society and its rulers in his books. The Catholic Church condemned his books, and the French Parliament banned them.

French author François Rabelais wrote satirical books that criticized religion and the government.

By the twentieth century, satire was a major theme in literature. Author George Orwell used it to critique modern society. His most famous work was *1984*. It showed the future as a bleak place. People lived under the watch of an authority called Big Brother. It monitored every action anyone took. The twentieth century also saw the dawn of film. Filmmakers from Charlie Chaplin to Stanley Kubrick used film to point out society's flaws.

Orwell's book *1984* was published in 1949.

Cartoons in this Danish newspaper criticized Islam, and many people protested in anger.

Modern Satire

Modern satire can have serious consequences. In 2005, Danish newspaper *Jyllands-Posten* published cartoons critical of Islam. The cartoons showed the Islamic prophet Mohammad as a terrorist. They sparked protests in the Islamic world. That anger fueled attacks on embassies, and people died during the attacks.

The internet, TV, and film all use satire for comical effect. Publications such as the *Onion* are almost entirely satire. So are satirical news programs such as *The Daily Show*. These programs use a real news format. They look and feel like a news broadcast, but they're written as comedy. Critics argue that they blur the line between real and fake news. This often leaves viewers confused about what is real.

From 1999 to 2015, comedian Jon Stewart (*right*) hosted *The Daily Show*.

FAKE NEWS SPREADS QUICKLY ON SOCIAL MEDIA.

   The rise of social media sites such as Facebook and Twitter has provided a new way for satire to spread. People like to post memes, which are often satirical. Social media has also become a way to spread satirical news videos and news stories. They're often shared or posted without context. This makes them a form of fake news, even if they were not designed to be that.

Real or Fake?

Is this story real or fake? See the Fake News Toolkit on page 29 to help you decide.

DAILY NEWS

THE BEST SELLING NEWSPAPER IN THE WORLD

No. 49,725

Today's Edition

National - World - Business - Lifestyle - Travel - Technology - Sport - Weather

Trump Predicts Downfall of Mainstream Media

According to President Donald Trump's official Twitter account, the news media will disappear when he's out of office. He predicted that their ratings would drop and then they'd vanish. He believes the desire for higher ratings strongly affects the way the media covers him and his presidency.

View from the top

Lorem ipsum dolor sit amet, Consectetur adipiscing elit. Vivamus sit amet odio id lorem blandit luctus. Vivamus placerat viverra lorem, Vestibulum consectetur nunc vel sem laoreet dignissim. Cum sociis natoque penatibus et magnis dis parturient montes.

Consectetur adipiscing elit. Vi-

The best way to get something done is to begin

Donec sed turpis ligula. Vestibulum vitae dignissim eros, quis scelerisque lectus. Donec blandit

"Morbi lobortis lacinia, elit in suspendisse egestis, ullamcorper ligula erat,

Economy

Vivamus est elit, tristique id sollicitudin id, mattis et dolor. Morbi lobortis lacinia elit in euismod.

Real! Trump's wild prediction got coverage from mainstream media sites. Researchers can verify the prediction by checking out his Twitter account.

Chapter 3

A HISTORY OF PARODY

Because parody is a form of satire, the history of parody and satire often go hand in hand. Some historians trace parody to ancient Greece. The term referred to a song or poem that imitated another. Greek playwrights also wrote parodies of tragic plays, making fun of their serious tone.

This ancient Greek carving shows Menander, a popular playwright of comedies.

Author Ben Jonson introduced the term *parody* to the English language in 1598. Parodies of that time included plays, songs, and novels. Some of them have become classics. For example, in the early seventeenth century, Spanish author Miguel de Cervantes published the novel *Don Quixote*. It is one of the most popular novels in history. Yet it is a parody of other romance novels of the era.

Ben Jonson wrote many comedic plays in England.

Columbia's Comedy Scoop of the Year!
THE THREE STOOGES
in
YOU NAZTY SPY

TRADE SHOW
Phœnix Theatre
TUES. APRIL 2ND

Any resemblance between

You Nazty Spy parodies leaders in Europe during World War II.

Modern Parody

By the twentieth century, parody had grown into a popular art form. In 1940, Columbia Pictures produced the film *You Nazty Spy.* The famous comedy team the Three Stooges played the roles of German and Italian leaders, including one character who looked like German dictator Adolf Hitler. It was an absurd slapstick comedy. But it also helped to raise awareness about the dictator.

More lighthearted parody grew popular in the second half of the twentieth century. *Monty Python and the Holy Grail* was a film parody of the King Arthur myth. Musician "Weird Al" Yankovic built a career creating sound-alike parodies of popular songs.

In the twenty-first century, parody news shows arrived. They use parody to make fun of politics and news. An example is *The Colbert Report* (2005–2014) on which Stephen Colbert parodied political talk show hosts.

Monty Python and the Holy Grail parodies the King Arthur myth.

Parody and Social Media

The internet and the rise of social media has given even more life to parody. For instance, online video sites such as YouTube are filled with parody. Several celebrity parody Twitter accounts have gone viral as well. Among them is the popular account @CaptAndrewLuck. It posts fake letters from football star Andrew Luck, writing as if he were a Civil War captain. The account has more than five hundred thousand followers. Even the real Andrew Luck is a fan.

Usually parody isn't created to cause confusion. It's made for entertainment and social criticism. But sometimes it crosses over into fake news. It's important to be aware of who is really behind a social media post.

Capt. Andrew Luck
@CaptAndrewLuck
Soldier. Colt. Simple man.

Tweets 471

This Twitter account parodies life during the American Civil War.

Real or Fake?

Is this story real or fake? See the Fake News Toolkit on page 29 to help you decide.

Anna Lopez
December 18, 2018

Have you all seen the amazing video that's making the rounds? You guys, it shows a plane coming in for a landing and it does a flip—like, a total 360! For real! About to fly to the Bahamas for winter break. Sure hope that doesn't happen on my flight!

Like   Comment   Share

Fake! Such a video really does exist. You can even Google it. But it was made on a computer. It fooled millions, though. How could you tell it's fake? The video was posted without context. The video showed only the flip. And no major media organizations carried it. Research into aeronautics quickly would reveal that such a flip and recovery is impossible.

Chapter 4

SPOTTING SATIRE AND PARODY

We live in an information age. From TV to newspapers to the internet, news is everywhere. But not all news is created equally. It is up to each of us to understand

what is real and what is not. Everyone should be a skeptic. That doesn't mean we should disbelieve everything. It does mean that we must learn not to accept everything we read or see as fact.

Don't believe everything you hear, read, or see!

Be a Skeptic

Usually, satire and parody are easy to spot. Creators aren't trying to fool anyone into believing it's real. But sometimes, a story meant to be satire is published out of context. When that happens, it's up to you to know how to identify it.

How do you do it? Suppose you see a story online. Ask yourself about the source of the information. Is it from a reliable source? Does the story include complete information? Does it seem like the writer's intent is to entertain rather than inform? If the answer to any of these questions is no, be skeptical.

If you see an unbelievable video, research it more to see if it is real.

The internet is a place where fake news can spread quickly. But it's also a place where you can do research. Does something about a story seem questionable? Get online and do a search. See if you can confirm a fact or story on a reliable, dependable website. Try to avoid sites that seem strongly biased or that make lots of wild claims.

Satire and parody are a part of our culture. They serve a useful role in providing entertainment as well as in raising social and political issues. As long as you know what they are, you'll be a step ahead in knowing what's real from what's fake.

Fact-based sites that you'd use for school research are good places to start when investigating a story.

Fake News Toolkit

When you watch or read a news story, it can be difficult to spot fake news. People want you to believe what they believe. Many try hard to convince you, even if they have to lie or twist facts. Read on to arm yourself with some tools for spotting fake news.

Consider the Source

Does the news come from a respected media source? News items that come from little-known sources are more likely to be fake. Learn about the organization that published the story. Is its purpose to provide fair, objective news?

Look for Objectivity

If an article tells only one side of a story, it might be fake news. A good news story should look at an issue from all sides and let readers come to their own conclusions.

Check the Facts

Don't just accept any information that a news story gives you. Follow up. Find out where the information comes from. Do the figures and surprising facts presented come with sources? And if they do, can you follow up on them?

Don't Spread It

If you see a story that you think might be fake news, don't spread it! Don't like it or share it. Don't even click on it. The best way to make fake news go away is to ignore it.

Report It

Google, Facebook, and many other websites now have buttons that allow you to report fake news. If you are sure an item is fake, report it. That can help stop the spread of the story and prevent it from fooling others.

Glossary

bias: prejudice for or against a person, group, or idea

context: the circumstances that form the setting for an event

criticism: the expression of disapproval for something based on its flaws or weaknesses

embassy: the official residence or office of an ambassador

ironic: using words, especially to be funny, that mean the opposite of what you really think

meme: a funny video, image, or short bit of text often created for and shared on social media

parody: a form of satire in which a work or image is imitated in an exaggerated, humorous way

satire: the use of humor, irony, exaggeration, or ridicule to expose and criticize social or political issues

skeptic: a person who questions or doubts ideas or opinions

skit: a short comedy performance, often using parody

social media: websites that allow users to create and spread content

viral: a story, video, or social media post that is quickly and broadly shared

Learn More about Satire and Parody

Books

Dakers, Diane. *Information Literacy and Fake News*. New York: Crabtree, 2018. What is fake news? How can you spot it? Learn more in this book.

Goldstein, Margaret J. *What Are Conspiracy Theories?* Minneapolis: Lerner Publications, 2020. Conspiracy theories are a different form of fake news you may encounter. Find out what they are and how they spread

Vink, Amanda. *Online Activism: Social Change through Social Media*. New York: Lucent, 2019. Social media is a powerful tool for social and political change. Learn more about how people use it to promote ideas and change attitudes.

Websites

BBC: Real versus Fake News
https://www.bbc.co.uk/academy/en/articles/art20180307163518942
Watch videos on this site that will help you spot fake news when you see or read it.

FactCheck.org
https://www.factcheck.org/
Is a story real or fake? Head to FactCheck.org for articles and statistics that can help you decide.

National Geographic Kids: How to Spot Fake News
https://kids.nationalgeographic.com/explore/ngk-sneak-peek/april-2017/fake-news/
This website offers tips for spotting fake news and advice on how to deal with it.

Index

Photo Acknowledgments

Image credits: Harry Hamburg/New York Daily News Archive/Getty Images, p. 4; Norman Ng UPI Photo Service/Newscom, p. 5; Andrew Harrer-Pool/Getty Images, p. 6; Bernhard Staehli /Shutterstock.com, p. 7; MCT/Getty Images, p. 8; PictureLux/The Hollywood Archive/Alamy Stock Photo, p. 9; Independent Picture Service, pp. 10, 24; Ben Rose/Getty Images, p. 11; DEA/G. DAGLI ORTI/Getty Images, p. 12; Dennis Jarvis/flickr (CC BY-SA 2.0), p. 13; Wikimedia Commons (public domain), p. 14; CBW/Alamy Stock Photo, p. 15; FRANCIS DEAN/DEAN PICTURES/Newscom, p. 16; White House Photo by Pete Souza, p. 17; pixelfit/E+/Getty Images, p. 18; bgblue/DigitalVision Vectors/Getty Images, p. 19; Dave & Margie Hill/Kleerup/Wikimedia Commons (public domain), p. 20; Library of Congress (LC-USZ62-116190), p. 21; Everett Collection, Inc./Alamy Stock Photo, p. 22; Archive Photos/Moviepix/Getty Images, p. 23; fonikum/DigitalVision Vectors/Getty Images, p. 25; Jose Luis Pelaez Inc/DigitalVision/Getty Images, p. 26; NetPhotos/Alamy Stock Photo, p. 27; Juice Images/Cultura/Getty Images, p. 28.

Cover: Robert Wallis/Corbis/Getty Images.